Wild Animal

MW00844700

RING-TAILED LEMURS

GAIL TERP

BLACK
RABBIT
BOOKS

Bolt is published by Black Rabbit Books
P.O. Box 3263, Mankato, Minnesota, 56002.
www.blackrabbitbooks.com
Copyright © 2018 Black Rabbit Books

Jennifer Besel, editor; Grant Gould, interior
designer; Michael Sellner, cover designer;
Omay Ayres, photo researcher

All rights reserved. No part of this book may be reproduced, stored
in a retrieval system or transmitted in any form or by any means,
electronic, mechanical, photocopying, recording, or otherwise,
without written permission from the publisher.

Cataloging-in-Publication Data is available at the Library of
Congress.
ISBN 978-1-68072-190-4 (library binding)
ISBN 978-1-68072-255-0 (e-book)
ISBN 978-1-68072-488-2 (paperback)

Printed in the United States at CG Book Printers,
North Mankato, Minnesota, 56003. 3/17

Image Credits
Alamy: A & J Visage, 27;
Duncan Usher, 4–5; Nigel Dennis,
20–21; Pete Oxford / Danita Delimont,
Agent, 21 (right); Tom Uhlman, 17; Zoonar/
Nadezhda Bolotina, 13, 26–27; Getty Images:
Wolfgang Kaehler, 31; iStock: nicolay, 14–15;
nixha2, 8–9; Shutterstock: Angyalosi Beata, 18;
Antero Topp, 3; Arto Hakola, 6–7; corlaffra, 1, Back
Cover; Deborah Lee Rossiter, 21 (left); Edward Hast-
ing-Evans, 11; Evgeniy Ayupov, 24 (insects); GUDKOV
ANDREY, 12; Jolanda Aalbers, 32; Le Do, 24 (flow-
ers); Lotus Images, 24 (fruit); Marcella Miriello, 23;
Natalia Paklina, 24 (lemur); Stephen B. Goodwin, 24
(snake); Stephen Mcsweeny, 24 (hawks); tratong,
Cover; Vladimir Wrangel, 28; National Geographic
Creative: Joel Sartore, 24 (fossa).
Every effort has been made to contact copyright holders for material reproduced
in this book. Any omissions will be
rectified in subsequent printings
if notice is given to the
publisher.

Contents

CHAPTER 1

A Day in the Life

It's morning. A **troop** of ring-tailed lemurs wakes up in a tree. The lemurs eat the tree's fruit. As they eat, they call to one another.

The lemurs make their way to the ground. Some look for more food. Others sit in the sun, soaking in the warmth. At noon, the lemurs stretch out on branches and nap. When they wake, they eat again.

Primates

Ring-tailed lemurs are **primates**. Primates are **mammals**. Apes and monkeys are primates. Humans are primates too.

These lemurs have gray fur. Their faces and bellies are white. But they are best known for their striped tails. The black and white rings make them easy to spot. Their long tails help lemurs balance while leaping through trees.

RING-TAILED LEMUR FEATURES

STRIPED TAIL

EARS

EYES WITH DARK RINGS

NOSE

FEET

SNOUT

HANDS

CHAPTER 2

Food to Eat
and a Place to Live

Ring-tailed lemurs mostly eat fruit. They eat tamarinds a lot. These juicy fruits grow on trees in long pods. Lemurs also eat leaves and flowers. They eat bugs too.

Ring-tailed lemurs are just one of more than 110 lemur species.

Home Sweet Home

Ring-tailed lemurs live only in Madagascar. They most often live in forests. Lemurs can survive hot and cold temperatures. Some live in areas that can reach 118 degrees Fahrenheit (48 degrees Celsius). Other lemurs live where it gets as cold as 5 degrees F (-15 degrees C).

Madagascar is an island off the coast of Africa. It's about the size of Texas. Most of the island's animals live only in Madagascar. They live nowhere else in the world.

Ring-Tailed Lemur Range Map

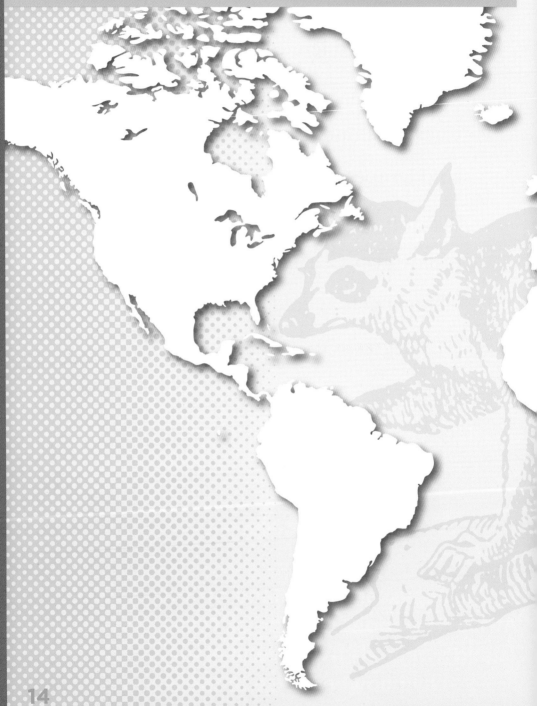

CHAPTER 3

Family Life

Ring-tailed lemurs live in troops. These groups have up to about 24 members. A female leads each troop.

Lemurs are very **social**. All members take part in **grooming**. They lick each other's fur. They also scrape the fur with toothcombs. Toothcombs are sets of six teeth. These teeth stick out from the animals' lower jaws.

Keeping in Touch

Ring-tailed lemurs use sounds to **communicate**. They bark and growl to warn of danger. They also scream and howl. Mothers purr when they are with their infants.

Lemurs use scent too. Lemurs' bodies make a smelly liquid. Lemurs use this liquid to mark where they live. They also use it to find **mates**.

Male lemurs have stink fights. They rub scent on their tails. Then they wave their tails at each other. They keep waving until one backs down.

By the Numbers

ABOUT 13
number of black rings on their tails

12 MILES
(19 kilometers) per hour

TOP SPEED

2014
YEAR RING-TAILED
LEMURS WERE LISTED
AS **ENDANGERED**

36
TEETH

16 to 19
YEARS
LIFE SPAN

Having Babies

Female ring-tailed lemurs give birth in late summer. Most often, they have one infant. Sometimes they have two.

About three weeks after birth, babies crawl onto their mothers' backs. They ride there often. When lemurs are six months old, they can take care of themselves. Females stay with their troops for life. Males move to other troops.

Comparing
Head to
Body Lengths

adult

newborn

4 INCHES
(10 cm)

inches 0   2   4

15 to 18 INCHES
(38 to 46 centimeters)

6   8   10   12   14   16   18

Ring-Tailed Lemur Food Chain

This **food chain** shows what eats ring-tailed lemurs. It also shows what these lemurs eat.

SNAKES

FOSSAS

HAWKS

RING-TAILED LEMURS

FLOWERS　　FRUIT　　INSECTS

CHAPTER 4

Predators
and Other Threats

Several animals eat ring-tailed lemurs. Fossas are catlike animals that hunt them. Snakes hunt lemurs too. Birds of prey, such as hawks, look for lemurs from the air.

Human Threat

People also hunt ring-tailed lemurs. They hunt lemurs for food. They also trap lemurs to keep as pets.

Humans are a threat to lemurs in another way. They cut and burn forests where lemurs live. The animals must find new homes.

Saving Ring-Tailed Lemurs

Ring-tailed lemurs are endangered. But people are taking steps to help protect them. They've set aside park land. These parks are safe places for lemurs. People have also passed laws to protect lemurs.

The number of lemurs is dropping. But people hope the parks and laws will save these amazing animals.

Endangered Lemurs
total: about 111 species

more than **80**% threatened with extinction

communicate (kuh-MYU-nuh-kayt)—to share information, thoughts, or feelings so they are understood

endangered (in-DAYN-jurd)—close to becoming extinct

food chain (FOOD CHAYN)—a series of plants and animals in which each uses the next in the series as a food source

grooming (GROOM-ing)—to clean and care for someone or something

mammal (MAH-muhl)—a type of animal that feeds milk to its young and usually has hair or fur

mate (MAYT)—one of a pair that joins together to produce young

primate (PRI-mayt)—any member of the group of animals that includes humans, apes, and monkeys

social (SO-shul)—liking to be with and talk to others

troop (TROOP)—a group of animals or people

BOOKS

Bell, Samantha. *Meet a Baby Lemur.* Baby African Animals. Minneapolis: Lerner Publications, 2016.

Gregory, Josh. *Lemurs.* Nature's Children. New York: Children's Press, an imprint of Scholastic Inc., 2017.

Schuetz, Kari. *Lemurs.* Animal Safari. Minneapolis: Bellwether Media, 2013.

WEBSITES

Ring-Tailed Lemur
kids.nationalgeographic.com/animals/ring-tailed-lemur/#ring-tailed-lemur-group-tree.jpg

Ring-Tailed Lemur
kids.sandiegozoo.org/animals/mammals/ring-tailed-lemur

Ring-Tailed Lemurs
www.nwf.org/Kids/Ranger-Rick/Animals/Mammals/Ringtail-Lemurs.aspx

INDEX